m.s.c.

ROTHERHAM PUBLIC LIBRARIES

Growing Up

Diane James & Sara Lynn

Illustrated by Joe Wright

TWO-CAN

Young & Old

All living things grow – people, plants and animals. Some grow quicker than others but they all need food. We eat food that comes from plants and animals. But plants have to make their own food. They use sunlight, water and air. We are going to look at the way people, plants and animals grow, and the changes that take place.

Babies

One of the first things babies do when they are born is cry. Until they learn how to speak, babies cry quite a lot. They may cry if they want something, such as food. Or if they are uncomfortable.

Very young babies do not need solid food. They take milk from their mothers, or from a bottle. When they are about 4 months old they start eating mushy baby food.

When a baby is a few months old, he may start to crawl, using his arms and legs to push him along. Later, he will start trying to pull himself up, using chairs and the legs of tables.

Babies like to watch things moving. Hang a mobile above a baby's cot and his eyes will follow the movement of the shapes. Babies also enjoy playing with brightly coloured toys.

Mobile

Get ready...
Coloured paper
Length of wooden dowel
  or a coat hanger
Cotton
Glue
Scissors

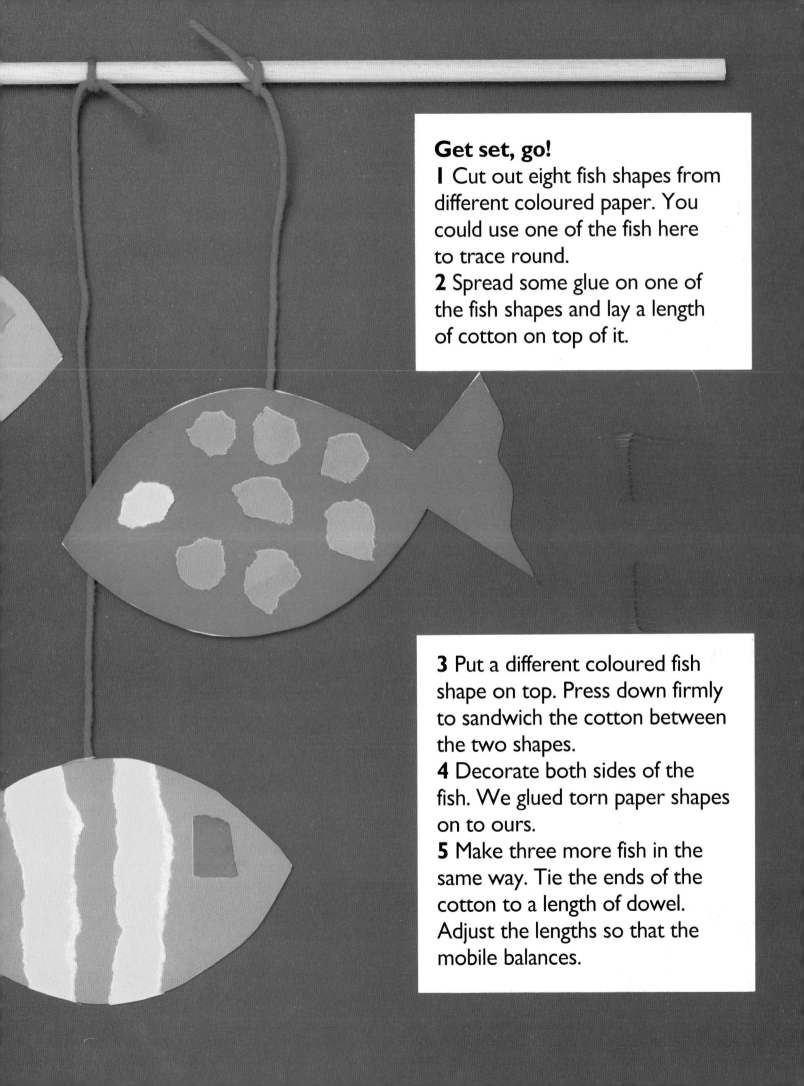

Get set, go!

1 Cut out eight fish shapes from different coloured paper. You could use one of the fish here to trace round.

2 Spread some glue on one of the fish shapes and lay a length of cotton on top of it.

3 Put a different coloured fish shape on top. Press down firmly to sandwich the cotton between the two shapes.

4 Decorate both sides of the fish. We glued torn paper shapes on to ours.

5 Make three more fish in the same way. Tie the ends of the cotton to a length of dowel. Adjust the lengths so that the mobile balances.

Early Days

Human babies learn to walk over a period of time. They often crawl on their hands and knees before they can balance on two feet! But some baby animals, such as foals, start walking as soon as they are born. They are usually a bit wobbly to start with!

Some baby animals do not look like their parents when they are born. Their fur or feathers grow later. They stay close to their mother or father for warmth and safety, just like the baby monkey here.

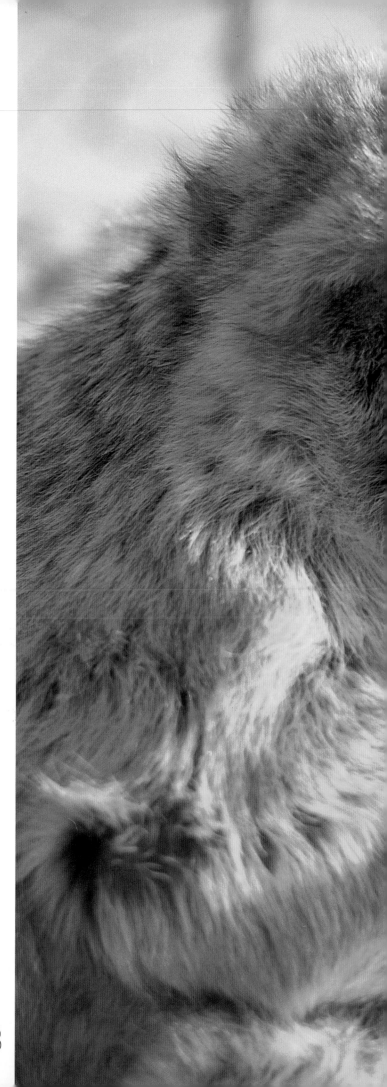

8

First Steps

When a baby is about 1 year-old she may start walking! At first, she will probably be a bit unsteady, and may fall over after one or two steps. This is when young children are known as 'toddlers'.

Toddlers learn through play. Simple toys, such as bricks, can help very young children learn about colours, shapes and balance. When toddlers start talking it is often difficult to understand what they are saying. They discover new words every day and soon learn how to put sentences together.

Toddlers can feed themselves and eat the same food as grown-ups. They often go through phases of liking certain foods more than others.

As toddlers get older, their balance improves. They can walk or run without falling over. At this stage, most toddlers are able to ride bicycles. Some toddlers go to playschool for a few hours each day. They start to learn their A, B, C, and to count up to 10. Most toddlers like painting and drawing and playing games of make-believe.

Letter Fun

Here is a great way to explore letters. You could make a letter picture for yourself, or as a present for a friend.

Get ready...
Coloured paper
Glue
Scissors

Get set, go!
1 Make a background for your letter picture. You could use a sheet of coloured card. Or stick sheets of coloured paper on to a piece of cardboard.

2 Cut, or tear, letters from coloured paper and glue them on to the background. They do not need to be perfect letter shapes!
3 Decorate the letters by gluing on torn paper shapes.

Mums & Babies

When baby animals are born they depend on their mothers for food in the same way as human babies. Some take milk straight from their mothers. Others wait until their mothers bring food to them.

Baby animals do not stay with their mothers for nearly as long as human babies. They often have to take care of themselves a few months after they are born.

Some animal mothers spend a lot of time cleaning their young. They lick them all over after meals. Human babies are bathed very carefully in warm water!

Many animals learn from watching their parents. They are taught to hunt for their own food. Their lessons are sometimes learned through play.

These young lion cubs are thirsty! They are safe from danger because their father is close beside them. The cubs have watched to see how he crouches down to get close to the water.

Off to School

One of the most important parts of growing-up is going to school. Most children go to school when they are about 5 years-old.

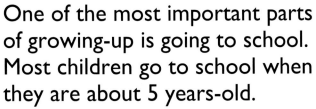

At school, children learn to read and write, and how to do maths. They also learn to look at what is happening around them, and to ask questions.

School is a good place to make new friends. As well as lessons, school children play games, practise playing music and singing, and put on plays for special occasions.

Most schools have three holidays each year – in spring, summer, and winter. Do you like holidays? What do you do?

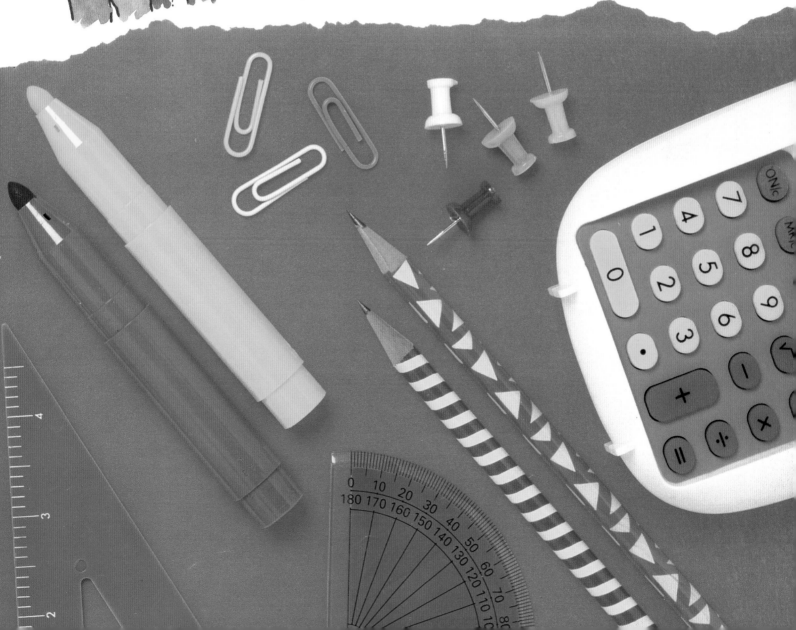

Height Chart

Make a height chart like the one here to measure yourself and all your friends.

Get ready...
Coloured paper
Glue
Scissors
Building block

2 Use a building block to measure strips of paper to stick along one side of the long strip. Glue them at equal distances apart, using the block as a guide. Decorate the centre of the height chart with a giraffe! You could use the one here as a guide.

Get set, go!
1 Start with a long strip of paper, about 1.2 metres long. You will need to join two pieces together.

3 Use a book to measure a friend's height. Count the number of sections below the book. Are you taller or shorter than your friend?

Teenagers

Between the ages of 13 and 19, young people are known as teenagers. These years are an exciting part of growing-up. Most children grow quite a bit taller during this period.

In mid-teens, most youngsters start thinking about what they would like to do when they leave school. They talk to their teachers, friends, and parents about it. Some children think they know what they want to do when they are very young. Do you know?

The teenagers in this dinghy are enjoying an adventure holiday. They are old enough to look after themselves and have fun with their friends. Older teenagers can learn to drive cars and make decisions for themselves about all sorts of things.

Look Alikes!

Have you noticed that you look like one or more of your relatives? You may have the same colour hair as your mum or the same colour eyes as your dad. Or, you may look more like your grandparents. Perhaps you look like your brother or sister?

Try to find a photo of your mum and dad when they were the same age as you. Do you look like either of them? Look at the picture of the family here. Do you think any of them look like one another?

The children in the picture above are twins. Twins are often born within minutes of each other. They usually look very similar, and sometimes they are almost identical!

Family Snaps

We have discovered that members of a family often look like one another. Here is a good way to put this to the test with your family!

Get ready...
Coloured paper
Scissors
Glue
Family photographs

Get set, go

1 Collect as many photos of members of your family as you can. If your mum or dad have brothers and sisters, you could include your aunts, uncles and cousins. Try to get photos of your grandparents and maybe their parents, too.

my mum's mum

my gran

my mum

me

my mum's dad

my dad's mum

my dad's dad

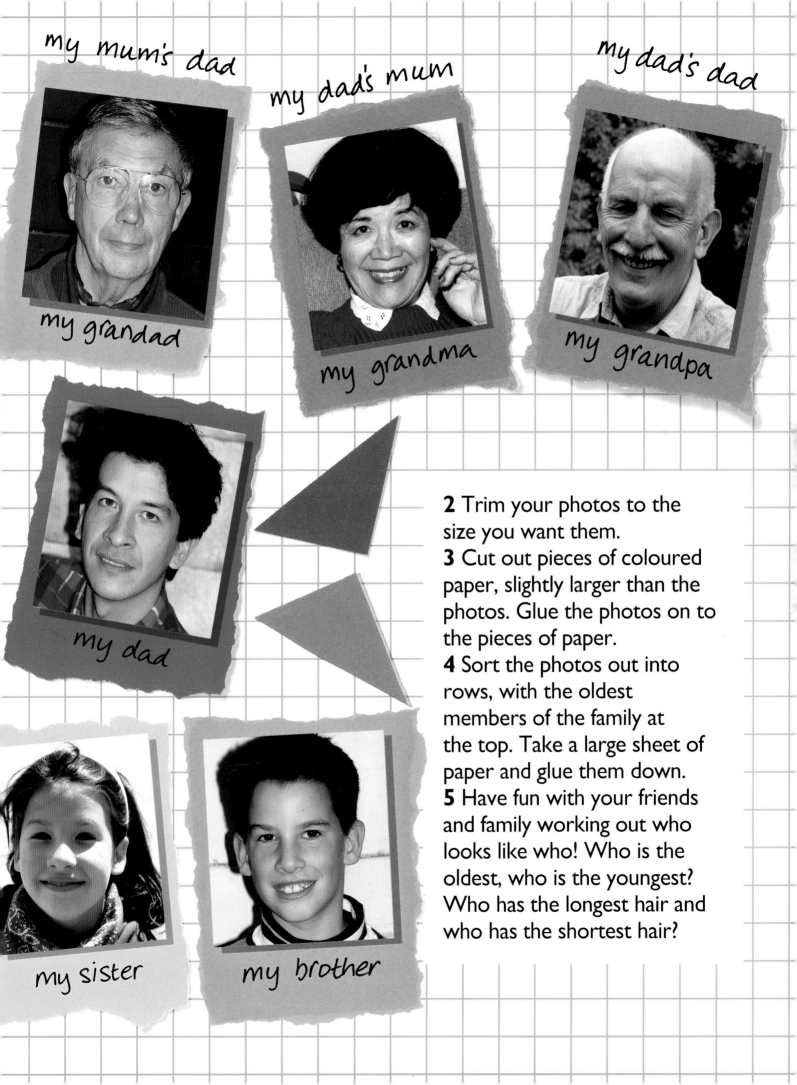

my grandad

my grandma

my grandpa

my dad

my sister

my brother

2 Trim your photos to the size you want them.
3 Cut out pieces of coloured paper, slightly larger than the photos. Glue the photos on to the pieces of paper.
4 Sort the photos out into rows, with the oldest members of the family at the top. Take a large sheet of paper and glue them down.
5 Have fun with your friends and family working out who looks like who! Who is the oldest, who is the youngest? Who has the longest hair and who has the shortest hair?

All Change!

Some animals change completely as they grow up. For example, who would believe that a tiny, wriggly tadpole could become a champion jumping frog.

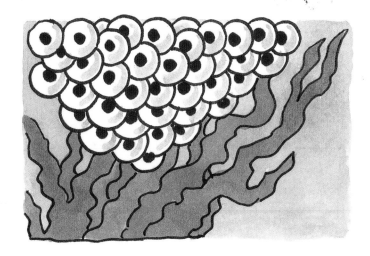

The newly hatched tadpole grows its back legs and then its front legs.

Female frogs lay their eggs in water. The eggs are called spawn. Spawn looks like clear jelly with a black spot in the middle. The black spot grows into a tadpole.

When the tadpole's lungs have developed, it can leave the water and breathe on land. Can you think of any other animals that look completely different when they grow up?

Watch it Grow

We have looked at how baby animals and humans grow. Now you can do a simple experiment to see how a plant grows. Most plants grow from seeds made by the parent plants. The bean on this page is the seed of a bean plant. Look at how the roots grow down and the shoot grows up.

Get ready...
Blotting paper
Broad bean seed
Jam jar

3 days

1 day

5 days

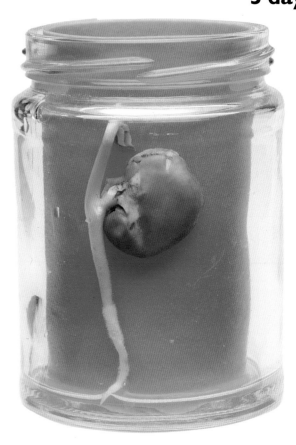

7 days

Get set, go!

1 Soak a bean in a saucer of water for a day.

2 Roll up a piece of blotting paper and push it into a jam jar.

3 Slide the bean down gently between the blotting paper and the side of the jar.

4 Pour enough water into the jar to make the blotting paper moist.

5 After a couple of days you will notice a tiny root appearing. Watch the bean carefully. A few days after the root appears you should see a shoot growing upwards.

9 days

11 days

Quiz

1 What is one of the first things a baby does when it is born?

2 What is this toddler doing?

3 When do babies start to crawl?

4 What is a tadpole called when it is grown-up?

5 When do toddlers start to walk?

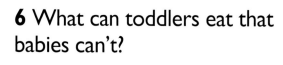
6 What can toddlers eat that babies can't?

7 What sort of things do young children learn at school?

Index

Question Answers

p26
Q. Can you think of any other animals that look completely different when they grow up?
A. Caterpillars to moths and butterflies. Maggots to flies.

p30-31
1 They cry.
2 He is playing with building bricks.
3 When they are a few months old.
4 A frog.
5 When they are 1 year old or more.
6 Toddlers can eat the same food as grown-ups.
7 They start to learn their A,B,C, and to count up to 10.

Photo Credits Cover, p. 6-7, p. 10-11, p. 16-17, p. 18-19, p. 22-23, p. 24-25, p. 28-29 Steve Shott; p. 2-3 Zefa; p. 4-5 © Fiona Pragoff; p. 8-9, p. 15 Planet Earth Pictures; p. 20-21 Bob Thomas Sports Photography; p. 27 NHPA

First published in Great Britain in 1994 by
Two-Can Publishing Ltd, 346 Old Street
London EC1V 9NQ
in association with Scholastic Publications Ltd

Pbk ISBN: 1-85434-231-2
Hbk ISBN: 1-85434-230-4

If you have enjoyed this book look out for the full JUMP! STARTS range

PLAY & DISCOVER What We Eat
◆ Rain & Shine ◆ What We Wear
◆ Growing Up
CRAFT Paint ◆ Paper ◆ Fun Food ◆ Dress Up
ANIMALS Pets ◆ On Safari ◆ Underwater
◆ On the Farm ◆ Animal Homes ◆ Birds

For more information about TWO-CAN books write to: TWO-CAN Publishing Ltd, 346 Old Street, London EC1V 9NQ